Trace your .

 I have _____ fingers on my hand.

 Circle the ones using their hands.

Draw the path to the nest.

  Count the dots.
Write the numbers.

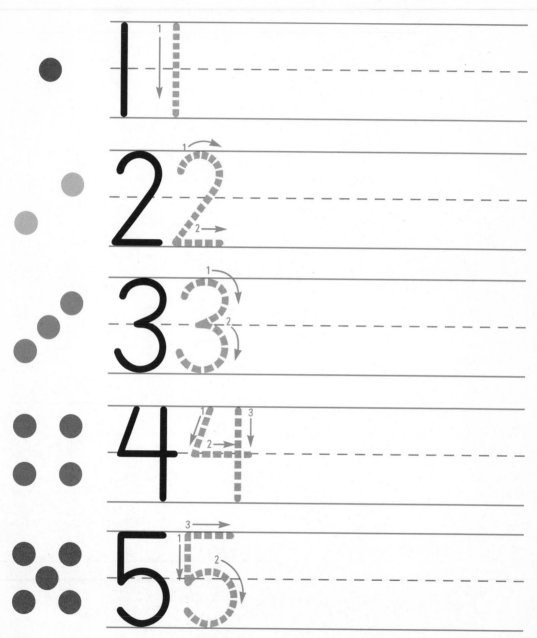

Count the stars.
Write the numbers.

 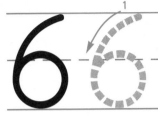

 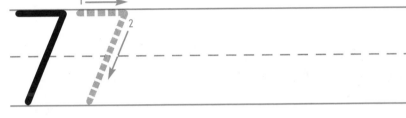

 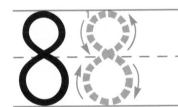

 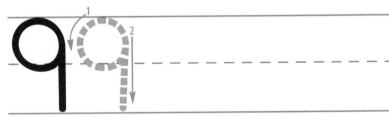

 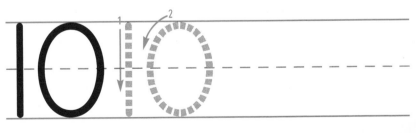

Draw the path to the pot of gold.

Find and circle the numbers in the picture.

Color the shapes with a ●.

8

Draw the path to the gingerbread house.

Connect the dots.
Color the picture.

Color the picture using the color code.

1 =   2 =   3 =

4 =    5 =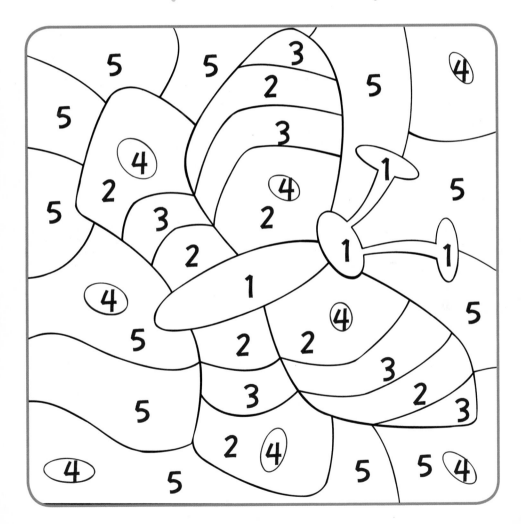

Connect the dots.
Color the picture.

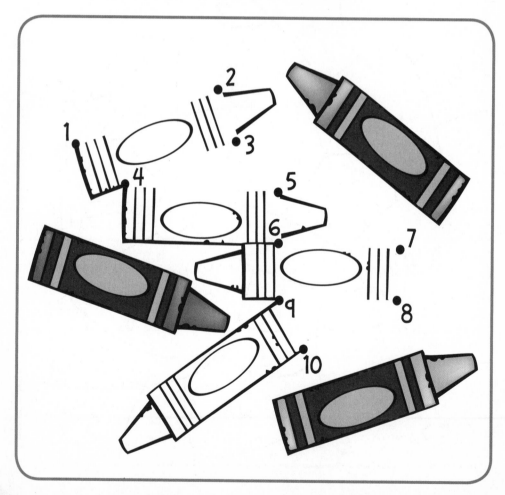

Make A Match

 Draw a line to the one that matches.

Mountain Maze

 Draw the path to the top of the mountain.

Circle the one that is different in each group.

Circle what doesn't belong.

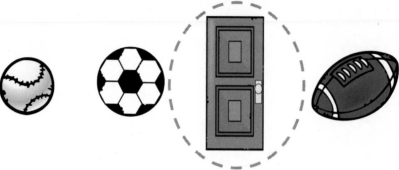

 Color the picture using the color code.

1 =   2 =   3 =

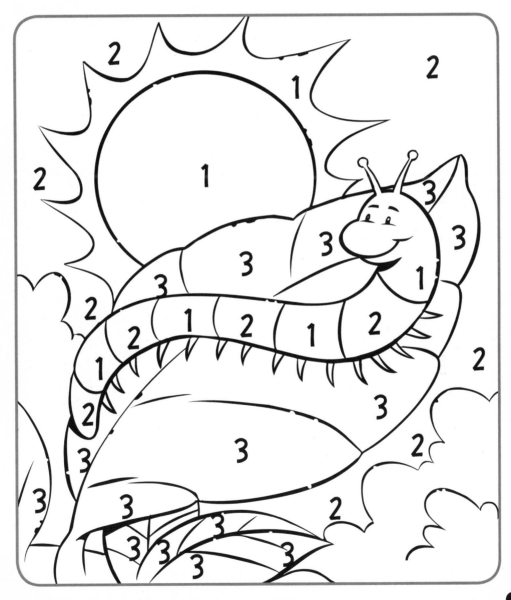

Draw a line to the one that matches.

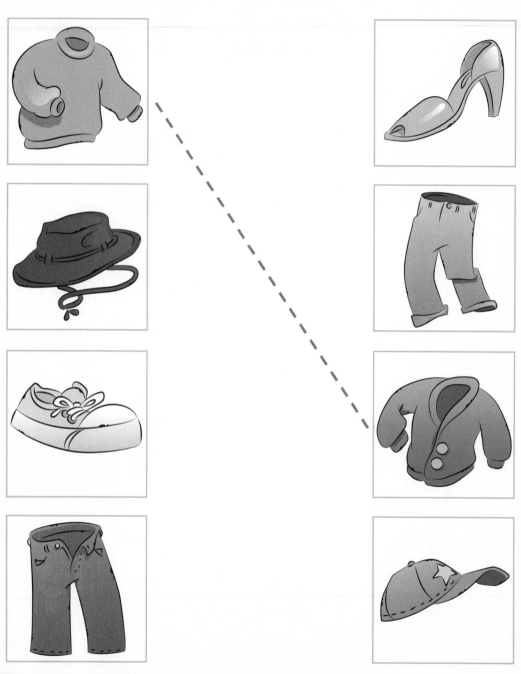

Circle the number
of items shown.

1　　　2　　　3　　　4　　　5

1　　(4)　　2

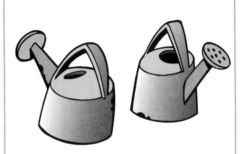

2　　　5　　　3

3　　　1　　　5

2　　　4　　　5

Circle the item that goes with the first one.

Give the Dog a Bone

 Draw a line from the dogs to the matching number of bones.

Color to show the number.

9	
7	
5	
10	
6	
8	

Count the sheep and write the number to show how many.

_____

- - - - - - - - - - - - - - - - - -

_____

_____

- - - - - - - - - - - - - - - - - -

_____

_____

- - - - - - - - - - - - - - - - - -

_____

_____

- - - - - - - - - - - - - - - - - -

_____

 Trace and write the numbers.

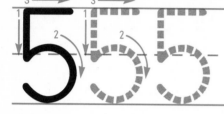

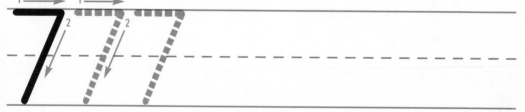

  **Trace and write the numbers.**

8

9

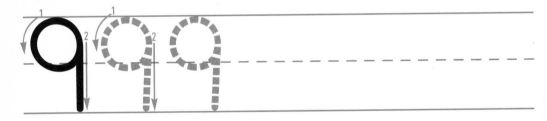

10

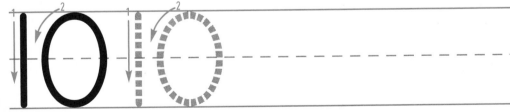

Count the flowers and
write the numbers.

_ _ _ _ _ _ _

_ _ _ _ _ _ _

_ _ _ _ _ _ _

_ _ _ _ _ _ _

_ _ _ _ _ _ _

_ _ _ _ _ _ _

_ _ _ _ _ _ _

_ _ _ _ _ _ _

_ _ _ _ _ _ _

_ _ _ _ _ _ _

Matching Food

 Draw a line to the one that matches.

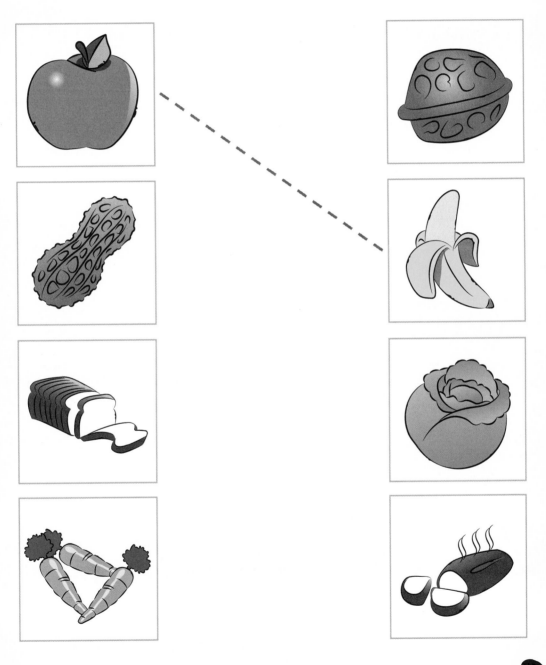

Trace the ◯s.

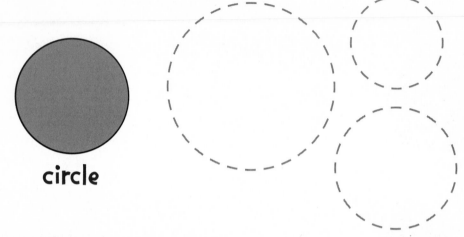

circle

 Color the ◯s.

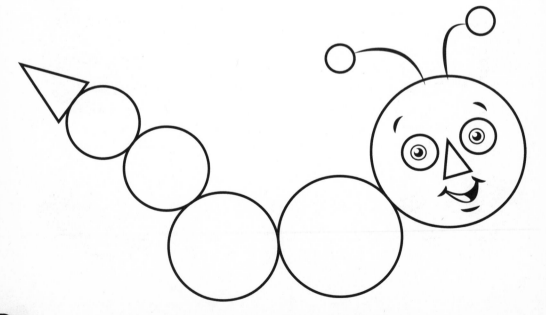

Color the O s.

Trace the ▢s.

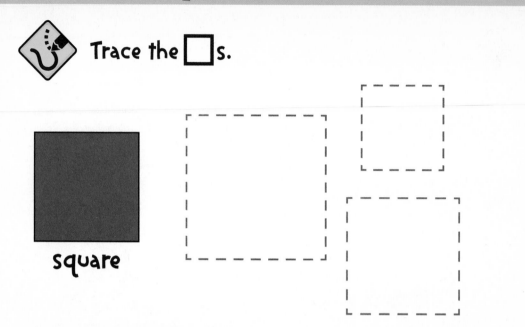

square

Color the ▢s.

Square World

 Color the ☐ s.

Trace the △s.

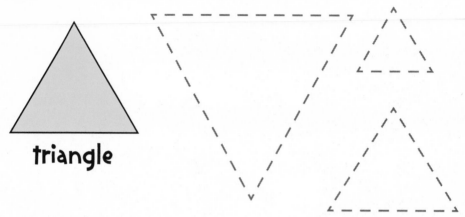

triangle

 Color the △s.

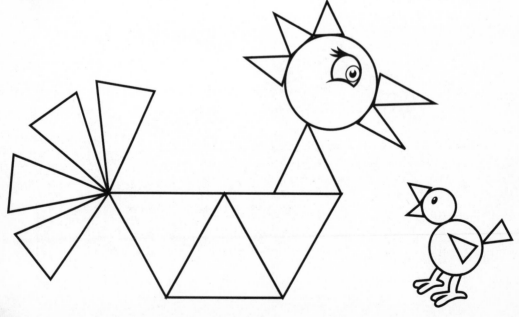

Color the △s.

Trace the ☐ s.

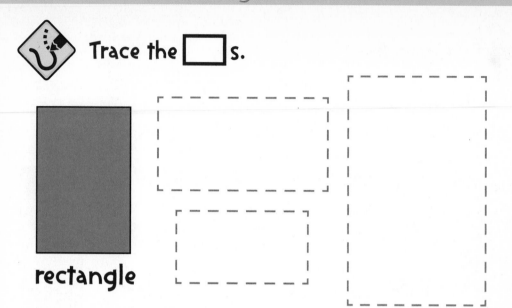

rectangle

Color the ☐ s.

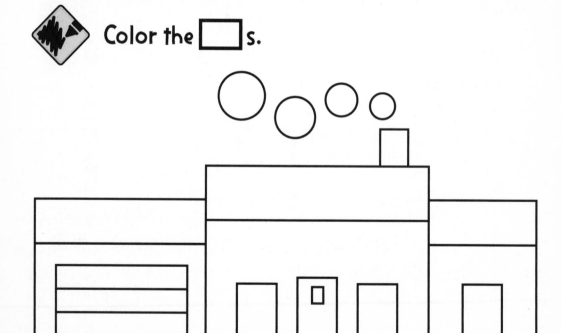

Color the ▭ s.

 Draw and color what comes next.

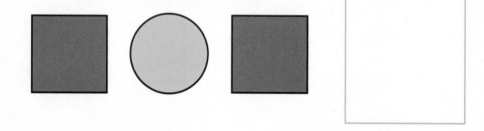

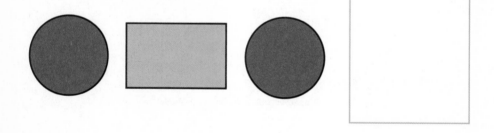

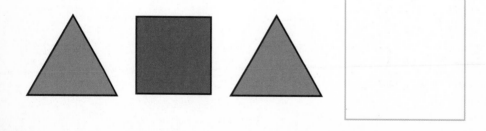

Circle the matching capital letters.

g
(G) H E

d
D B A

e
C E A

a
A G E

f
C H F

b
E B C

h
G B H

c
C F G

Circle the matching capital letters.

i

N (I) P

k

K M J

o

L N O

j

I J K

x

K X M

n

M O N

l

P L K

p

L P K

m

M O N

Circle the matching capital letters.

s

| Z | (S) | U |

q

| Q | R | X |

u

| V | U | W |

w

| U | V | W |

z

| Z | S | X |

t

| Y | S | T |

y

| X | Y | U |

r

| R | T | Z |

v

| V | U | W |

 Connect the dots from 1 to 26.
Color the picture.

Draw the path to the elephant.

41

 Connect the dots from A to Z.
Color the picture.

Find and color the letters PIG.
Color the rest of the picture.

Read the rhyming words.

cat   hat   bat

  Trace the beginning letter. Draw a line to the matching picture.

ram

jam

 Color the one that rhymes with ram.

 Color the ones that rhyme.

Read the rhyming words.

jet   wet   pet

 **Trace the beginning letter.
Draw a line to the
matching picture.**

jet

wet

pet

pen

ten

 Color the one that rhymes with pen.

 Color the ones that rhyme.

Read the rhyming words.

pin   fin   chin

  Trace the beginning letter or letters. Draw a line to the matching picture.

pin

chin

fin

king

ring

Color the one that rhymes with king.

Color the ones that rhyme.

Read the rhyming words.

log

frog

jog

 Trace the beginning letter.
Draw a line to the
matching picture.

jog

og

frog

clock

sock

 Color the one that rhymes with clock.

 Color the ones that rhyme.

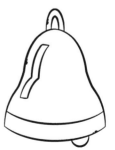

Read the rhyming words.

mug   rug   bug

  Trace the beginning letter.
Draw a line to the
matching picture.

 rug

 mug

 bug

drum

plum

 Color the one that rhymes with drum.

 Color the ones that rhyme.

more

fewer

 Circle the one that shows more.

 Circle the one that shows fewer.

It's a Party

Circle the set in each row that shows **more**.

 Circle the set in each row that shows fewer items.

sad

happy

 Color the sad rabbit .

Color the happy rabbit .

in

out

 Color the dog in the doghouse .

Color the dog out of the doghouse.

big

little

Color the big house .

Color the little house .

59

up

down

 Color the balloon that is up.

Color the balloon that is down.

long   short

Color the long bench .

Color the short bench .

Color the shapes using the color key.

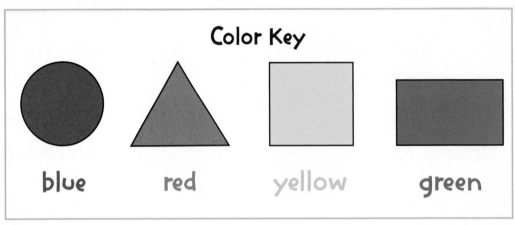

Color Key

blue red yellow green

Colored Shape Patterns

 Draw and color what comes next.

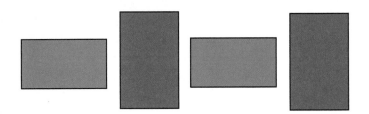 

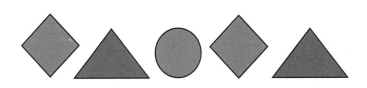 

Find and circle the animal names in the box.

 ANT

 BIRD

 DUCK

 HEN

 DOG

 FISH

H	D	O	P	C	A	V	O	T
I	U	N	H	E	N	E	N	F
V	C	E	N	H	B	V	E	I
C	K	S	D	R	I	O	S	S
C	A	N	T	Z	R	O	T	H
T	R	S	R	H	D	O	G	N